Harry Potter Knock Knock Jokes for Kids

The Unofficial Book of Funny Laugh-out-Loud
Harry Potter Knock Knock Jokes

Written by: Nina Riddle

Harry Potter Knock Knock Jokes for Kids: An Unofficial Harry Potter Book

HARRY POTTER KNOCK, KNOCK JOKES

Knock, knock

Who's there?

Troll

Troll who?

Troll in the dungeon, just thought you should know!

Knock, knock

Who's there?

Wand

Wand who?

Wandering through the neighborhood and I thought I'd say hello.

Knock, knock

Who's there?

Quidditch

Quidditch who?

Quidditch'ing that rash or it's never gonna heal.

Knock, knock

Who's there?

Parselmouth

Parselmouth who?

You gotta learn Parselmouth if you want a job at FedEx.

Knock, knock

Who's there?

You-Know-Who

You-Know-Who who?

Yeah I know Hu-Hu, she's a great Quidditch player.

Knock, knock

Who's there?

Alchemy

Alchemy who?

Algimme these theater tickets because he's sick with the flu. You wanna come with me?

Knock, knock

Who's there?

Bill Weasley

Bill Weasley who?

Bill Weasley for all the stuff he broke. And if he doesn't pay up then we'll fine Gryffindor another 50 points.

Knock, knock

Who's there?

Hogsmeade

Hogsmeade who?

Hogsmeade a huge mess in the barn. I'll pay you one Galleon to clean it up.

Knock, knock

Who's there?

He-Who-Must-Not-Be-Named

He-Who-Must-Not-Be-Named who?

What did I just say!?

Knock, knock

Who's there?

Ron

Ron who?

Ron for your life, the Death Eaters are coming!

Knock, knock

Who's there?

Wizard with a time-turner

Wizard with a time-turner who?

Sorry I have no idea what you're talking about.

Knock, knock

Who's there?

Winky

Winky who?

Winky so I know you haven't been petrified by the Basilisk.

Knock, knock

Who's there?

Wormtail

Wormtail who?

Wormtrail has gone cold. I'm afraid we're never gonna catch this guy.

Knock, knock

Who's there?

Wise

Wise who?

Wizengamot is filled with crotchety old bats.

Knock, knock

Who's there?

Coffin

Coffin who?

Coffin up a storm here because of all this dust. You should get a broom and clean the Chamber of Secrets.

Knock, knock

Who's there?

My tent

My tent who?

My Tentacula escaped from its cage. You haven't seen have you? Wait never mind don't turn around. Everything is going to be okay. Whatever you do, make sure you don't sneeze.

Knock, knock

Who's there?

Annie

Annie who?

Annie Magi, and I can turn into a skunk. So you better not mess with me or it's gonna be a stinky night in London.

Knock, knock

Who's there?

Dumbledore

Dumbledore who?

Well if you're not going to answer me, then I'll just have to kick down this dumb-old-door.

Knock, knock

Who's there?

Butter

Butter who?

Butterbeer for sale, how much you want?

Knock, knock

Who's there?

Alecto

Alecto

Alecto the right mayor or those potholes will never be filled.

Knock, knock

Who's there?

Erith

Erith who?

Arithmancy is the ancient study of the magical properties of numbers, duhhh. I can't believe you didn't know that.

Knock, knock

Who's there?

Wise

Wise who?

Wizengamot is filled with crotchety old bats.

Knock, knock

Who's there?

Auror

Auror who?

Sure Voldemort is pretty bad, but if you ask me Dolores Umbridge is the real h-auror around here.

Knock, knock

Who's there?

Tonks

Tonks who?

Tonks for nothing, Muggle!

Knock, knock

Who's there?

Aloha

Aloha who?

Alohamora, welcome to Hawaii, do you need help unlocking your suitcase?

Knock, knock

Who's there?

Severus

Severus who?

Severus over in accounting were wondering if you wanted to go for lunch?

Knock, knock

Who's there?

Who who

Who who, who?

I don't know want to be mean but your owl accent is terrible.

Knock, knock

Who's there?

Boggart

Boggart who?

Boggart is smelly and gross and I won't have it hanging in my living room next to my nice paintings.

Knock, knock

Who's there?

Dragon

Dragon who?

Dragon and on why don't you?

Knock, knock

Who's there?

Dursley

Dursley who?

Durs-leeks in my soup and I didn't order because I don't like vegetables so take it back or I'll turn you in rat.

Knock, knock

Who's there?

Ava

Ava who?

Avada Kedavra!

Knock, knock

Who's there?

Sirius

Sirius who?

Sirius about buying a dragon? Better get some oven mitts.

Knock, knock

Who's there?

Gaunt

Gaunt who?

Gaunt you see I'm working? Go away and leave me alone!

Knock, knock

Who's there?

Griphook

Griphook who?

All you need to fish for goblins is a Griphook and sinker.

Knock, knock

Who's there?

British Bobsled Team

British Bobsled Team who?

I can't believe you haven't heard of us, we were in the movie *Cool Grunnings*.

Knock, knock

Who's there?

Gryffindor

Gryffindor who?

Gryffindoor is for Griffins not for students. Hufflepuff loses 20 points!

Knock, knock

Who's there?

Vampire

Vampire who?

You know, the vumpire you ordered to referee the baseball game.

Knock, knock

Who's there?

Veela

Veela who?

Veelanguising around all day and it's not very productive so let's go outside why not?

Knock, knock

Who's there?

Flutterby Bush

Flutterby Bush who?

Flutterby Bush and smell the roses.

Knock, knock

Who's there?

Freezing Charm

Freezing Charm who?

Freezing ch'arms off if you go outside in that sleeveless sweater.

Knock, knock

Who's there?

Death Eater

Death Eater who?

Death Eat-here sometimes but he stopped coming when they banned him from bringing in his scythe.

Knock, knock

Who's there?

Deflating

Deflating who?

Deflating on the stove is a cursed frying pan. Don't touch it if you value your fingers.

Knock, knock

Who's there?

Skrewt

Skrewt who?

Skrewt came loose on my chair and I fell over. Can you fix it?

Knock, knock

Who's there?

Bow

Bow who?

Beauxbatons Academy of Magic sent an owl for you, did you get it?

Knock, knock

Who's there?

Moody

Moody who?

Moody cows of yours just broke my fence and it's gonna cost four Sickles and eight Knuts to fix it. So pay up!

Knock, knock

Who's there?

Mudblood

Mudblood who?

Mudblood is what you get when you fight a wizard war in the middle of a swamp.

Knock, knock

Who's there?

Lumos

Lumos who?

Lummos and carrot sticks is a healthy snack. You make it using it chickpeas, also known as garbanzo beans which is a much cooler name.

Knock, knock

Who's there?

Keeper

Keeper who?

Keeper away from me, I hate that girl!

Knock, knock

Who's there?

Umbridge

Umbridge who?

Ummm, bridge washed away in the hurricane. So how are we gonna cross the river?

Knock, knock

Who's there?

Unicorn

Unicorn who?

Unicorn? As in one corn? What am I supposed to do with a single head of corn? There's a start-of-term feast in four hours!

Knock, knock

Who's there?

Toad

Toad who?

Toadtally not a good idea to drink that potion you just found. Most of them do terrible things.

Knock, knock

Who's there?

Triwizard

Triwizard who?

Triwizards accomplish more than try-not wizards.

Knock, knock

Who's there?

The Knight Bus

The Knight Bus who?

The Knight Bus will get you home okay, but it stops running at midnight. After that you need take a taxi or a vroomstick.

Knock, knock

Who's there?

Professor Kettleburn

Professor Kettleburn who?

Professor Kettleburn'ing, quick someone cast Aguamenti before he burns the school down!

Knock, knock

Who's there?

Flamel

Flamel who?

Flamel burn down the cabin if you don't put it out.

Knock, knock

Who's there?

Floo

Floo who?

No, no, it's "Floo where?" Who is for people.
Where is for destinations. How did you not know
that? Did someone use a memory charm on you?

Knock, knock

Who's there?

Hedwig

Hedwig who?

Yeah that's about what she sounds like. Have you seen her around?

Knock, knock

Who's there?

Elixir

Elixir who?

E lixir face and then says, "It's not my fault I look like a dog, I drank the wrong potion!

Knock, knock

Who's there?

Ronan

Ronan who?

Ronan around outside and just wondering if you wanted to join me.

Knock, knock

Who's there?

Portkey

Porkey who?

Portkey students will be placed on a diet of salad and lean meat.

Knock, knock

Who's there?

Hit Wizards

Hit Wizards who?

Hit wizards and they will hit back. Same with witches. Really you shouldn't be hitting anybody. What were you thinking?

Knock, knock

Who's there?

Honeydukes

Honeydukes who?

Honey dukes once a week down at the goblin boxing gym. She's really great at it.

Knock, knock

Who's there?

Slytherin

Slytherin who?

Slytherin through the woods is a Basilisk. Don't look him in the eyes or you'll be a corpse.

Knock, knock

Who's there?

Rowling

Rowling who?

Rowling the boat is tough work but did you know there's a spell for that? The Rowboat Spell will cause small watercraft to propel itself forward.

Knock, knock

Who's there?

Dementor

Dementor who?

Dementor trains the apprentice but in the Star Wars movies they always go bad.

Knock, knock

Who's there?

Diagon

Diagon who?

Dia-gone to the alley to me buy some floo powder and she never came back!

Knock, knock

Who's there?

Ravenclaw

Ravenclaw who?

Ravenclaw my eyes out so I'll need to see the nurse, please.

Knock, knock

Who's there?

Remembrall

Remembrall who?

Remembrall all the good times we had playing Quidditch?

Knock, knock

Who's there?

Foe-Glass

Foe-Glass who?

Foe-Glass on your studies if you want to pass your exams.

Knock, knock

Who's there?

Newt Scamader

Newt Scamader who?

New Scam-out-there works like this. Someone sends you an email claiming to be the Headmaster of Hogwarts and you've won a million Galleons in the lottery. Hang up immediately. Never give your goblin banking information out over the phone and you'll be safe.

Knock, knock

Who's there?

Comet

Comet who?

Comet to a one-year subscription of *Which Broomstick?* and I'll throw in this jar of cat hair.

Knock, knock

Who's there?

Crabbe

Crabbe who?

Crabbe me a soda if you're going to the kitchen.

Knock, knock

Who's there?

Pure-Blood

Pure-Blood who?

Pure-Blood is something only a vampire would drink. So get that outta my face before I throw it in yours!

Knock, knock

Who's there?

Nagini

Nagini who?

Na,gini can't make you fall in love with someone. Or grant you more wishes, or raise a corpse from the dead.

Knock, knock

Who's there?

Buckbeak

Buckbeak who?

Buck'a'beak is as low as I can go. Anything less and I'd be losing money.

Knock, knock

Who's there?

Nox

Nox who?

Nox'ing on the door all morning and nobody answered so I went home and made a baloney sandwich and now I'm back.

Knock, knock

Who's there?

Mandrake

Mandrake who?

Man, Drake's new album is Bombarda Maxima.

Knock, knock

Who's there?

McGonagall

McGonagall who?

Wow did you the Beater smack that Bludger? That ball is McGonagall.

Knock, knock

Who's there?

Seeker

Seeker who?

Seeker out by the vending machines if you want to buy some dragon liver.

Knock, knock

Who's there?

Shacklebolt

Shackleboltwho?

Shacklebolt and lock the door after I leave. I feel a disturbance in the Force.

Knock, knock

Who's there?

Minerva

Minerva who?

Minervas are shot and I don't think I'm getting enough sleep. Think there's a potion for that?

Knock, knock

Who's there?

Myrtle

Myrtle who?

Myrtle cracked his shell. Do you think we should take him to the veterinarian?

Knock, knock

Who's there?

Sickle

Sickle who?

Sickle and flu can be cured with a potion, but it's easier to use healing magic.

Knock, knock

Who's there?

Slug club

Slug club who?

Slug clubs for sale! Who wants to bash some slugs?

Knock, knock

Who's there?

Expecto Patronum

Expecto Patronum who?

You should probably ask for something better than an owl.

Knock, knock

Who's there?

Expelliarmus

Expelliarmus who?

Sorry, you've been disarmed, so I'll be asking the questions here. Now where did you hide the Goblet of Fire?

Knock, knock

Who's there?

Potter

Potter who?

Potter or pan, what's the difference? I'm not using it to make breakfast, I wanna smack somebody.

Knock, knock

Who's there?

Polyjuice

Polyjuice who?

Probably-juice is what they're gonna serve but it's a Muggle funeral so all bets are off.

Knock, knock

Who's there?

Diggle

Diggle who?

Diggle little bit over near the giant X and maybe we'll find buried treasure.

Knock, knock

Who's there?

Divination

Divination who?

Divination has replaced radio nation but now it's losing ground to Netflix.

Knock, knock

Who's there?

Dobby

Dobby who?

Dobby ridiculous, of course there's such a thing as elves.

Knock, knock

Who's there?

Albus

Albus who?

Albus look both ways before crossing the road so you don't get hit by a Ford Anglia.

Knock, knock

Who's there?

Crookshanks

Crookshanks who?

Crook shanks a guy the locker room and only gets two years. I cast one lousy unforgiveable curse and they sentence me to Azkaban.

Knock, knock

Who's there?

Werewolf

Werewolf wh—

Where wolf? I have no idea, but there's a vampire right behind you.

Knock, knock

Who's there?

Harry

Harry who?

Harry up or we're going to be late for the football game.

Knock, knock

Who's there?

Remus

Remus who?

Remus-t visit The Wizarding World of Harry Potter at Universal Orlando. You wanna drive or take a fireplace?

Knock, knock

Who's there?

Centaur

Centaur who?

Seen-tower in the forest and it's tall and dark and I wonder what it does.

Knock, knock

Who's there?

Charm

Charm who?

Charm tired from waving that wand around all day?

Knock, knock

Who's there?

The Blood Baron

The Bloody Baron who?

The Bloody Baron the back porch wants a bandage for his paw.

Knock, knock

Who's there?

Draco

Draco who?

Draco too much soda before the movie and I had to run outside the use the bathroom but I don't like the bathrooms at the theater so I broomed over here to your place and how about letting me in now because I really gotta go.

Knock, knock

Who's there?

Fat Friar

Fat Friar who?

Fat fryer won't fit in the kitchen so I dunno how we're gonna make these chicken wings.

Knock, knock

Who's there?

Seamus

Seamus who?

Seamus-t go down when the tide goes out.

Knock, knock

Who's there?

Firebolt

Firebolt who?

Firebolt so fast through the house I thought I was a goner. Thank goodness the fire department arrived so quickly.

Knock, knock

Who's there?

Flitwick

Flitwick who?

Don't flitwick or the candle will go out.

Knock, knock

Who's there?

The Chamber of Secrets

The Chambers of Secrets who?

Sorry I don't give out that sort of information. It's not called the Chamber of Explanations after all.

Knock, knock

Who's there?

Binns

Binns who?

Binns are full so please take out the trash!

Knock, knock

Who's there?

Bulstrode

Bulstrode who?

Bullstrode through the china shop and killed all the teapots.

Knock, knock

Who's there?

Canary

Canary who?

Can-Harry stop by later to help me clean Fluffy's dog bed?

Knock, knock

Who's there?

Paracelsus

Paracelsus who?

Paracelsus some of those acid pops and cockroach clusters. We've got a party to get to!

Knock, knock

Who's there?

Pettigrew

Pettigrew who?

Pettigrew plenty potted purple plants. (*Try and say that five times fast.*)